LET'S GET THIS POTTY STARTED!

The BabyShrink's Guide to Potty Training Your Toddler

BY DR. HEATHER WITTENBERG

LET'S GET THIS POTTY STARTED!

The BabyShrink's Guide to Potty Training Your Toddler

BY DR. HEATHER WITTENBERG

A babyshrink BOOK

Let's Get This Potty Started!

The BabyShrink's Guide to Potty Training.

Heather Wittenberg, Psy.D.

Published by BabyShrink, LLC, United States of America. Let's Get This Potty Started! The BabyShrink's Guide to Potty Training Your Toddler. © 2013 by Heather Wittenberg, Psy.D.

This book is for informational purposes only, and is not meant as an evaluation or treatment of medical or psychological conditions. Please contact your health care professional for specific information about your child or family's health.

ISBN 978-0-9886835-0-1

For more parenting advice, helpful discussions, and to be notified when Dr. Heather's next book is released, sign up for her newsletter, Shrinky Thinks, at www.BabyShrink.com.

"All of us have moments in our lives that test our courage. Taking children into a house with a white carpet is one of them."

—ERMA BOMBECK

CONTENTS

"Usually the triumph of my day is, you know, everybody making it to the potty."

—JULIA ROBERTS

WELCOME!

There's a huge divide in our country, and I'm not talking Republicans and Democrats. I'm talking parents and nonparents. Nonparents run screaming from the room when a baby spits up on their cashmere sweater. Parents scrape vomit out of the back seat with their bare hands. Nonparents can fly First Class. Parents change diapers in car trunks. Nonparents go out to dinner...at 9:00 p.m. Parents? We have purses filled with fruit snacks, Goldfish crackers, plastic spoons and Barbie Band-Aids. The two groups can coexist, but if you're reading this book, I'm guessing you're a parent. And my props to you, because it's not glamorous. But it is meaningful, challenging, and occasionally hilarious.

No parenting phase, however, feels more like work than the process of potty training. Just when you thought your life was about to get easier and less expensive, potty training can shred your patience and lay waste to your expectations. It can be repetitive, messy and frustrating. But you can do this! I'm here to help you and your family on the road to a potty-trained kid. Come, let's go together. Wait, you have a Goldfish stuck to your shoulder. There. Okay, now we're ready.

ABOUT ME

I'm a psychologist with four young children, two boys and two girls. My husband and I changed diapers—nonstop—for eleven straight years. Each of our children has asserted his or her independence in potty training in completely different ways. We've experienced super-easy, super-early training; super-challenging, super-late training; and everything in between. Along the way, we've tried every potty-training method known to man (or mom). Here's my conclusion: None of them work. And—all of them work. How can this be? Because your child is the variable that none of them take into account. Different methods work for different children. The "cha-ching!" perfect technique will vary both by age and by temperament. A simple approach might work best with a young toddler of nineteen months, while an older toddler, like a three-year-old, might need a more sophisticated plan. A spirited, spunky child may require a different approach than an "easy" child.

One of the most important lessons I learned in my doctoral studies is the power of individual differences. We humans simply aren't "One Size Fits All" creatures. The key to success in potty training is working with your child's personality, not against it. Despite what you may have heard, there's simply no

"Toilet training is the signature achievement for children this age."

surefire way to potty train your child. It's going to be a learning curve for both of you. If you keep that in mind, everyone will get through this journey a lot easier.

Children who have a good, positive toilet training experience are more likely to have greater self-confidence, feelings of self-control, and overall sense of achievement. Toilet training is the signature achievement for children this age. When you look at it this way, potty training your child is actually kind of an honor. YOU get to help him on this path. It may be rocky, it may be littered with a turd on the rug here and a puddle o' pee there, but it's an important path, and you get to walk it with your child, encouraging him and helping him discover his own success.

But it's not easy. I wrote this book because potty training is, by far, the most common concern raised by my readers at my website, BabyShrink.com. I launched the website in 2008 as a way to connect with parents who were dealing with the very same issues my husband and I struggle with in our own home. I also have the insights I've gotten via my doctoral degree, in-depth training and years of clinical experience, and wanted to share those with other moms and dads. And I also wanted to reassure parents that their challenges aren't unique— even those of us licensed to deal with small children can get stumped. While my site addresses a whole range of parenting concerns, potty training always generates the most questions. This book answers many of these, but if you have more, you can always connect with me at BabyShrink.com on my Potty Page, via Twitter @BabyShrink, or on Facebook.

Now, a little about you, dear readers: You may notice that in this book I'm addressing a pair of parents ("mom" and "dad") who are married ("your husband", "your wife"). But parenthood comes in all shapes and sizes, married and un-, single and double. Potty training can be a little bit easier if you have a same-sex role-model available, but single dads of daughters, single moms of sons, military moms of sons whose husbands are deployed, and all other family combinations out there – this book is for you, too. You can do it, and I salute you!

Dr. Heather's Potty Training Cheat Sheet

If you need "quick and dirty" help with potty training your child, here's my cheat sheet. If you're starting this process, it can be helpful to print it out and post where you'll see it:

● Go at your family's pace
Don't let an external pressure—such as preschool entrance or an upcoming birthday—rush the potty training process for your child.

● Follow your child's lead
Wait until you see the signs of readiness, and back off if your child isn't yet interested.

● Different strokes for different wee folks
A child's personality type is a huge factor in determining which potty training methods work best.

● No shame games
Your positive, relaxed attitude toward potty training sets a great foundation for your child's self-esteem.

● Take a seat
Teach boys to use the potty sitting down. Standing up and aiming into the toilet is a skill that can come later.

- ◆ **One of the biggest causes of potty-training problems is… Constipation.**
  Pump up the fruits and veggies, and talk to your pediatrician for help, too.

- ◆ **My kid still wets at night!**
  This is a big problem, right? No, it's just reality. There are anatomical and neurological reasons children have a harder time staying dry at night.

- ◆ **Accidents happen**
  If you're toilet training a toddler, here's one must-have accessory: a zip-top plastic bag with a spare pair of undies and pants.

- ◆ **Don't be so hard on yourself**
  It's fine to go back to diapers or pull-ups for car rides, plane trips, or any other situation that calls for little extra security and convenience.

- ◆ **Hang in there**
  It may feel like it's taking a decade to potty train your toddler, but we promise, you'll get there. Potty training is a journey that can last days, weeks, months, even years. Pace yourself!

CHAPTER 1

THE BASICS: HOW (AND WHEN) TO START POTTY TRAINING

"A child can go only so far in life without potty training. It is not mere coincidence that six of the last seven presidents were potty trained, not to mention nearly half of the nation's state legislators."

—DAVE BARRY,
American writer and humorist

ARE WE THERE YET?

No matter what Grandma says, there is no perfect time to start potty training. A small percentage of children will be fully trained before they are 24 months old. These potty prodigies tend to be easy babies who are ahead of the curve in terms of their physical and intellectual development. They can understand—and follow—your requests, and want to make you happy; plus they haven't yet hit the era of defiant behavior so common with older toddlers. (And preteens. And teens. But all things in good time!) If you've got one of these super-early learners, by all means make the most of the opportunity and follow your child's interest in potty training. But don't fret if your child isn't among these rare few. Everyone has their strengths, right? Your "average" potty trainee certainly has other—uh—assets. My most challenging child to train is now a math whiz. (And besides, the endless potty training puns you encounter during this time will help keep you entertained.)

Most children make the leap around their third birthday.

Most children make the leap around their third birthday. Sometimes potty training only takes a few days, but more often, the process will last weeks or months. Another not-so-small percentage of children won't be trained until after they are three-and-a-half.

Boys tend to take a few months longer than girls, but this is only on average. Many boys master their skills early and quickly, just as many girls may take longer and struggle more. Your child's gender isn't as much a factor as his or her readiness.

REAL-LIFE QUESTION:

"Why isn't my kid showing ANY signs of potty training readiness?"

Most children show signs of readiness around age two, but it may take some detective work on your part to find the clues. Perhaps your son has become fascinated with the kitty doing her business in the litter box. Or maybe he loves to accompany Dad to the bathroom. Perhaps he's started to grab himself when he needs to go, or ducks behind the couch when it's time to "reload" his diaper. Maybe *Everyone Poops* is his new favorite book.

Once you've recognized these signs, follow his lead. Talk about the kitty using her box. Encourage Dad to keep up the bathroom bonding. Make a neutral observation if you see your son grabbing himself, or disappearing like he's about to drop a deuce behind the sofa. Don't rush ahead of his interest level and hustle him straight to the potty. Read his signals. If he's interested in taking the next step, he'll respond positively to your suggestions. If he doesn't, back off and try again next time.

If there are still no signs of potty readiness by age three, check with your child's pediatrician, since there are many medical issues—or language and other developmental delays—that can slow down the process of potty training. Notice that I said "no signs of potty readiness" rather than "completely potty trained," because the third birthday truly is an arbitrary potty-training cutoff.

NO DIAPERS? NO, SERIOUSLY. PEOPLE DO THIS.

The latest from the crunchy-granola fringe of the American parenting world is the conviction that babies can—and should—be potty trained early. Really early. As in: from birth.

When I first heard about this trend, I dismissed it as just that: A trend. Everyone knows that tiny little weeks- or months-old babies can't be potty trained.

Well, it turns out that more than half the world's babies are toilet trained before their first birthdays, according to Contemporary Pediatrics magazine. That's because in developing countries, diapers—whether disposable or cloth—are either ridiculously expensive, difficult to find, or completely nonexistent. There are no washers and dryers, and often no running water. No baby wipes. No fancy potties that play songs when Junior pees. No Diaper Genies or potty training apps. It's common in Africa,

Asia, India, and other developing parts of the world. Parents whistle or make a "swooshing" sound, to both encourage the baby to pee, and to create a conditioned trigger in the future for going. Mothers learn to read their babies' body language to discern when a pee or a poo is coming. Babies typically grimace, grunt, or grow distracted when it's time to go. Just like Daddy! But I digress. This doesn't mean tiny babies can remove their onesies, get to the potty, do their business, wipe, flush, wash their hands, and get dressed on their own. I wish. You'll still have to teach them all of that when they're toddlers. But the successful practice of what's being called "elimination communication" here in the United States does mean that with constant— and I mean 24/7—adult support, babies can learn to release their bladder and bowel contents on cue.

Training toddlers any time after 18 months is a very recent American approach.

Even in the U.S., immigrant families from developing countries tend to potty train their children much younger than people who have lived here longer. Training toddlers any time after 18 months is a very recent American approach. Remember that up until the 20th century, we were a developing country, too.

So if this is something you want to try from the time your child is an infant, go for it. But if the challenges start to outweigh the benefits for you, give yourself a break. In the culture we live in, there is plenty of time to be potty trained. And for those of you planning on tackling potty training any time after the age of, say, 18 months, stick with me, kid.

FIRST STEPS

Once your child is showing signs of readiness, you can buy a potty, perhaps shop for undies, or look at potty books together. Offer to let your toddler hang out with you or your partner in the bathroom while you're doing your business, and start to give a running commentary on readiness steps you observe. For instance, if you see him holding his crotch, in that classic "I need to wee!" pose, comment on it. "I notice that you are grabbing yourself. Maybe you have to go pee-pee?" Some children will complain of a tummy ache when they have to go. When you observe this, mention that it seems like pee-pee or doo-doo is coming, and remind them it's okay and when they use the bathroom, the hurt will stop. But don't bombard your child with directions—or shove the potty under them like a catcher's mitt. The natural oppositional state of toddlers will guarantee pushback.

GET THIS POTTY STARTED! SIGNS OF READINESS

So how can you get your child ready to potty train? Short answer: you can't. Children's bodies get themselves ready, on their own time. Your job is to wait for the signs, recognize them when they occur, and then help them walk—you can't carry them—along the road to potty freedom. Here are some common signs of readiness to look for:

- Pulling at a wet or dirty diaper

- Hiding to pee or poop

- Interest in others' use of the potty, or copying their behavior

- Having a dry diaper for a longer-than-usual time

- Awakening dry from a nap

- Telling you that they're about to go, are going, or have just gone in their diaper.

Once you observe some of these behaviors, you'll know it's time to move forward with your potty training adventure. But please: Set your expectations aside, and let your child drive the process. Society, and often our families, have strong expectations about potty training: We expect smooth and quick progress. The reality is usually much more complicated. If you're disappointed when your child doesn't meet overly high, "Now you're dry!" expectations, she may absorb your feelings and turn them into a sense of shame and inadequacy.

Children—even babies—are highly tuned in to our non-verbal communication. And shame is one of the worst feelings anyone can experience.

Potty training is like making a roast: Slow and easy is the recipe for success. (This is actually the recipe for many parenting challenges!)

Potty training is like making a roast: Slow and steady is the recipe for success.

NUMBER 1 OR NUMBER 2?

Most children will learn to pee in the potty first, but it's certainly not a requirement. Many children will master pooping in the potty first; it just depends on your child's anatomy and personality. So observe your child's behavior and follow her lead. Hey, if you can get her to put anything in the potty, you're making progress.

CHAPTER 2

POTTY PSYCHOLOGY 101

"Children thrive when parents set before them increasingly difficult, but always meetable challenges."

—UNKNOWN

POTTY MOUTH: THE LANGUAGE OF THE LOO

Do you say doo-doo or poopie? Tinkle or wee-wee? Penis or pee-pee? Vulva or jay-jay? The words your family uses to name private parts are personal—and important. It doesn't matter which words you use; every family has its own potty language. The more natural the words are for you, the more comfortable your child will feel. Pee-pee, tinkle, wee-wee, piddle, or *shi-shi* (the Japanese children's word we use where I live, in Hawaii) are all just fine. Some experts advise parents to always use the technical, anatomically correct terms for body parts and functions. While I agree that it's important for children to learn the proper names for our body parts, I disagree that it's necessary for us to use technical expressions, such as "having a bowel movement" or "do you need to urinate?" every time.

The more natural the words are for you, the more comfortable your child will feel.

Language specialists know that children learn better from grownups when we use words they can easily say and remember. And what's the big deal, anyway? We don't insist that Junior use technical language in other aspects of his life, so why should this rule apply to body parts? Why should he be able to call a train a "choo-choo," but not be able to refer to his penis as his "winkle"? That's no fun! Part of the joy of raising children is the silliness—the crazy kitchen dances we do, the good-night tickles or the unique words that make up our family traditions. Using silly words can help make sometimes tedious and challenging caretaking tasks, like helping a small child use the toilet, a lot more fun for both parent and child.

But what's more important than the actual words we use is how we say them.

But what's more important than the actual words we use is how we say them. Using a humiliating, belittling, or aggravated tone of voice with your potty trainee may result in a child who feels a sense of shame and embarrassment about her body, regardless of the actual words we say. Adopting a communication style that is matter-of-fact and accepting will convey comfort and confidence to your child. So go ahead and use whatever reasonably appropriate names you want for body parts and functions—all the better if your child helps to create them. It's OK if your child's preschool or babysitter uses different words than you do, if they say "piddle" and you say "pee," as long as your child is comfortable using those words. It helps for everyone to know each other's words, of course.

Whatever potty vocabulary you choose, here are the key things you will want to discuss with your child:

1) Everyone has to go sometimes,

2) What it feels like when you have to go,

3) And what to do about it.

There's actually a good reason for all this potty-talk: Giving your child words for her elimination-related feelings and experiences helps her learn how to think about her own body's inner workings, which then helps her reinforce the developing nerve pathway between the mind and the voluntary muscles that control toilet training. Therefore, the more potty talk, the better. If your child seems intrigued by the bathroom, but isn't chatting you up about it yet, that's okay. She will gradually absorb—sorry, toilet-paper pun!—the information. But if a kid is truly not interested yet, she isn't interested. Better to hold off on your efforts for now.

Over the years, I've come across lots of silly words used in potty training, and I will use them interchangeably in this book for your inspiration. Enjoy!

PERSONALITY AND POTTY TRAINING: WHAT TYPE IS YOUR CHILD?

As with many things in life, your child's temperament—her personality—will drive much of the learning process in potty learning. For example, a very active toddler might be difficult to slow down long enough to train easily. A child who resists anything new might cling to his diapers for dear life. Or a fiercely independent type might not be motivated until she realizes that potty training is one more thing I can do myssef! Based on the research on personality types in young children, and on my own clinical experience working with small fry, there are three toddler personalities that seem to be most common. Here is my version of them:

THE ACCOUNTANT

This child wants to learn the rules. Careful and meticulous, she always wants to do things the right way, and is motivated to follow your directions. But look out: Accountants can get rigid, obstinate, and resistant if you push too hard.

Accountants are usually hard-working children who strive to make their parents happy. They respond well to clear expectations. They want to know the plan for moving forward. They like to work toward rewards—a sticker, a check mark on their chart, the chance to buy panties with Rapunzel on them—especially if they get to help pick the rewards. Help your Accountant learn about the potty by going through the process one step at a time, and encouraging your child for accomplishing each step along the way. Accountants tend to like those "potty timers" that go off every 30 minutes or so to remind them it's time to try. But if you sense any resistance, back off—your Accountant will become rigid and negative if you push too hard.

THE HIPPIE

"Let it all hang out, baby!" Parents of this child worry he'll never be interested in potty training and just hope they can get the task done before she heads to college. Right now, he's too busy with toys, friends, and food to take notice of the load in his pants. Hippies are often the last to be potty trained, because they couldn't care less about it. They've got flowers to inspect, a ball to throw, and chocolate milk to slurp. Who has time for the potty, especially when it's so convenient to go right in your diaper?

Who has time for the potty, especially when it's so convenient to go right in your diaper?

Try not to get too frustrated with your little Hippie. This type of child is more easily trained when you wait and start the process later, saving everyone a lot of aggravation in the meantime. Hippies can often be talked into using the potty when they're a bit older (age three to three-and-a-half) and can better understand and appreciate your rationale. And you'll make better progress if the bathroom is stocked with fun things to do while he's going.

THE MULE

Nervous and resistant to anything new, this personality type likes things to stay just as they are. Suspicious of these newfangled pull-ups and all this talk of underpants, your Mule is cautious and worried about new challenges like potty training. The good news is, Mules often grow up to be persistent, creative, and fiercely loyal.

But in the meantime, give a lot of reassurance to your little Mule. Think of all the changes that come at a young child every day. "Daddy is picking you up today instead of Mommy." "The sitter is coming over." "We're going to a different park." We expect them to just roll with it, but it can be overwhelming for a young child. Mules are very observant and notice every little thing that changes in their environment—and it can make them feel insecure. Sometimes, your little Mule is just trying to hang on to some semblance of a predictable life, and diapers have been a big part of it so far. Gradual exposure is key for Mules. Nonchalantly introduce a potty to the bathroom. Give them time around it. Have them spend a few minutes without a diaper to see how it feels. Allow Mules to witness the rest of the family's bathroom habits. But don't get too pushy, or your Mule will balk.

POOH-POOH THE POWER STRUGGLE: LEAD BY FOLLOWING

In most areas of your child's life, YOU are the boss. You decide most of her daily happenings. But her bodily functions are different—you can't control those. After all, you can pick up a child who has run out into the street and put her into time-out. You can separate children who have gotten into a scuffle. But you can't force a child to eat, poop, or sleep. And in these areas, parents must tread very carefully. You want her to feel in charge of her own body, right? So back off and let her learn at her own pace.

If your child is resisting your potty training efforts, feels too stressed about your potty training approach, or is simply not ready, he or she may demonstrate this by refusing to use the potty. Or your child may use the potty at day care or preschool, but refuse to try at home. That's your cue to disengage from the power struggle you've inadvertently entered into. I know this won't be easy, but it's worth it because this kind of power struggle is very likely to emerge again in other areas. Tell him you're sorry for pressuring him about the potty, and that from now on, HE can decide where he poops and pees. It's HIS body. Take a deep breath, don't scold, and don't get emotional about it. He'll know if you're faking it. Let go of whatever expectations you've had, and let him drive this process. That doesn't mean he gets to be the boss in every area—far from it. But there's really no way for you to win this battle, and lots of ways you can make it worse for everyone. Take three deep breaths. Disengage.

A child who resists us can trigger strong feelings in parents. We are supposed to be the boss. We're paying the mortgage, we're buying the Goldfish, and we're used to being in control! There's something about an oppositional toddler that really makes us nuts. But getting into a power struggle with your toddler is guaranteed to work against you. Your child is deeply driven to develop a sense of autonomy in the world. Potty training, believe it or not, is one of the major ways she develops that. If we interfere, that sense of inner control and competence can be undermined.

Take three deep breaths.

Disengage.

Forcing a child to potty train by using threats, punishments, or other coercive methods will eventually backfire. If your child is doing the deed for you (or for his teacher, or Grandma or someone else), he won't internalize that sense of control and success. He won't feel that it's his body—his accomplishment.

Where does that leave us, the hapless parents? We must lead—by following. If that means your daughter busts out the Big Girl Panties for two weeks and then suddenly regresses back into diapers, so be it. If that means your son is peeing in the potty like a good soldier but refusing to poop in it until age 3 ½, so be it. Be thankful that you can buy pull-ups and wipes in bulk, and let it go. Psychologically, you're doing the right thing.

FINDING YOUR INNER GOLDILOCKS: HOW TO USE PRAISE—AND WHEN NOT TO

It can be hard for Mom or Dad to figure out how much praise they should lavish on their toilet trainee. In generations past, parents were taught not to praise their children, but today, we know that there are serious drawbacks to a cold, negative approach to child rearing. Inadequate praise leaves a hole in a child's heart; it makes him feel unnoticed and unloved. Many of us were raised in stoic households, and we don't want to withhold affection or kind words from our own children.

But as often happens, we've overcompensated as a society and now run the risk of praising our children too much. You can, in fact, overdo it on the praise, with serious and negative consequences. Excessive praise sets parents up for an unsustainable, ever-growing mountain of expectations. Every new accomplishment requires more fanfare than the one before. Rewards get bigger and more impressive, and the next thing you know, you're engraving a seven-foot trophy and renting a bouncy castle for every good deed your child does. Don't get stuck in that cycle.

The other problem is that excessive praise and "helicopter parent" hovering can undermine your child's own sense of motivation. Your child thinks, "If Mom and Dad make such a big deal out of this, maybe I'm doing it for them—not me."

You want to aim for the Goldilocks balance: Not too much praise, not too little praise, but just right. You'll best find this sweet spot by observing your child's reaction to your accolades. Genuine, low-key, specific praise works best. Don't just yell out, "Wow! Great job!" Instead, make an observation about the skill your child just demonstrated. "This time, I see you held your pee until you got to the potty. Nice job." Finding the right balance of praise is also a way to be respectful of your child's growing sense of mastery and independence. That way, the praise is about her actions, not our own needs.

What about the use of rewards, rather than praise, to encourage potty training? I know a family who gave their daughter an M&M for every time she peed in the potty, and three M&M's for every poop. This, uh, "sweetening of the pot," style of incentive can help, depending on the child and the personality, but I think there's too much focus put on rewards for potty success in the general parenting press. My easiest-trained child is my fourth, and we got in the habit of giving her a few mini-marshmallows each time she pooped in the potty. But she never needed them—she ended up learning fast and with no complications. Now she still expects the marshmallows, even though she's been trained for months! We created a mini-marshmallow monster, for no reason. (I'm not a pushover, though; I've drawn the line at making bathroom S'mores.)

Kiddos are deeply, internally motivated to master their bodies' own workings, and the rewards are fine—they sometimes help a lot—but just as often, they make the child think they're potty training for the prizes, rather than getting that genuine feeling

**NOTHING
often works
better than
SOMETHING.**

of self-mastery. The other drawback is that rewards often result in temporary progress. When the excitement of the prize wears off, you get regression. Then the parents are left trying to dream up bigger and better incentives—again resulting in temporary success—the unsustainable cycle. So the parent is left with the common complaint that "nothing works!" Nothing does work, actually. NOTHING often works better than SOMETHING. Ooh, a koan. An existential piddle riddle. And you just thought you were here for potty training help.

CHAPTER 3

HANDY TIPS AND TRICKS

"You can learn many things from children. How much patience you have, for instance."

—FRANKLIN P. ADAMS

WHAT TO WEAR, WHAT TO WEAR...

Convenience, cost, and personal preference are all valid things to consider when deciding whether to use pull-ups, underwear, diapers, or the eco-friendly plastic/cloth reusables. Start with your first preference, and see how your child does. If she's not making any progress after a few weeks, feel free to experiment with other options.

Some parenting experts advise you to pick one type of undergarment and to stick with it for the sake of consistency. My opinion? Consistency in general is important, but rigidly staying with a method that doesn't seem to be working just doesn't make sense. Especially if you are traveling—and going out for the day with a toddler counts as "traveling," since it requires nearly as much equipment and planning as summiting Mount Everest.

Consistency in general is important, but rigidly staying with a method that doesn't seem to be working just doesn't make sense.

Feel free to make things easier on yourself. You can use pull-ups, which can be easily slipped on and off in a mall bathroom, your car, on the side of the road, or anywhere else you may find yourself with a small person hollering, "I have to go pee-pee! Uh-oh!" Speaking of which, you don't go anywhere without an extra pair of pants for your toddler, do you? A "potty training pouch"—a zip-top plastic bag with a pair of spare pants and extra pull-up—can be a lifesaver. Stash one in the car, the diaper bag, your purse, and at your mother-in-law's house.

Most children will also cope just fine if you shift between putting them in diapers and pull-ups. However, if your child has a strong preference, it's worth it to go with what she prefers for the sake of progress. You can always re-introduce the other option, like underwear, again in a few weeks.

Potty training calls for simple clothing.

Potty training calls for simple clothing, so now is a great time to go through your kid's clothes and set aside the overalls; anything with a million snaps; long princess dresses; and superhero capes—just until the messy work portion of the training is completed. Because there's nothing more annoying than not getting your princess on the throne in time due to a bunch of pesky buttons, or accidentally draping her sparkly train into the poopie pot. How about some stretchy, no-fuss, elastic waist pants? And hey, those will work great for the kids, too. But seriously, the more your child can participate in the act of getting clothes on and off, the more she'll feel she's an important part of the process. This is especially important at day care, where the childcare providers often don't have time to tend to complicated outfits. Yes, I'm talking to you, Little Miss Leotard with Tights.

"GOT A MEETING IN THE LADIES' ROOM…"

I hope you're comfortable with your kids intently watching your every move in the bathroom—peeking behind you, handing you toilet paper, and even judging what you've deposited in the bowl—because this is one of the most powerful ways children can learn to be potty trained. Ah, parenting. Let go of notions like privacy and dignity, if you haven't already, and let your child see how the pros use the john. Be matter-of-fact about how it all works, answer questions, and talk about how good it feels to get all the poop and pee out of our bodies. Older siblings can be good role models too; just be sure to supervise the Big Kid if they are helping the Little Kid.

KID-SIZE POTTY OR TOILET INSERT?

Many children are delighted to receive their own little freestanding potty. First, it's toddler-sized, and not as intimidating as our big adult size toilet. Your child may enjoy that he can get himself on and off of a small potty without help. Second, it doesn't do shocking, loud things, like flushing, swirling, and filling. And finally, it's HIS. Another excuse to yell: Mine, all mine!

But a solid minority of toddlers prefer to use a toilet insert. Often, these children have older siblings they want to emulate. Or, they simply like climbing up and down the step stool to use the toilet. If you're one of the lucky parents whose child likes to use the regular toilet with an insert, go with it! You get to dodge the yucky task of scraping out a poopie little pot. But one word of caution: Don't pressure your child to use the insert if he has no interest. You don't want to risk a negative experience on the big toilet, which will be much harder to remedy later on. For example, children sometimes slip inside the bowl, or are unstable getting on or off the big toilet, making them afraid of trying again. Better to stick with the little potty until more experience and confidence have developed.

Another trick to try is the "backsplash" method: Have your child (girl or boy) sit backward on the toilet (with no insert). This position creates more stability, and if you have a boy, will allow your son to hold his penis down without difficulty. Little girls love this position too, because it's comfortable and feels less precarious.

TAKE A SEAT, BOYS!

It's true: By and large, boys take longer to train than girls do. But there are plenty of exceptions to this rule. So don't go into this process assuming your boy will be difficult to train. That said, unless you have a urinal in your home, I don't recommend having your son stand to pee until he's older. Peeing while standing up takes considerably more coordination and skill than peeing while seated. And peeing and pooping often happen at the same time, so if he's already sitting down, you might get a twofer. Dads, take one for the team and demonstrate for your son how to pee sitting down. (Unless you promise to clean up after your little shooter. Every time.) It's only for a short while, I promise.

You'll want to train your son to hold his willy down while sitting so that you don't get sprayed with pee every time he goes. At first, you'll have to help him. Another glamorous parenting task! But yes, get in there and help him, even if he is using a toddler potty that has one of those "pee shields" that supposedly do the trick for you. Often, they don't. Better to get him in the habit from the beginning. Over time, ask him to help and soon he'll be ready to take it over as HIS job.

> **Helping your child understand her body's internal "poop cues" can be a challenging, lengthy process.**

THIS IS THE POTTY YOU'RE LOOKING FOR: TODDLER MIND-READING TRICKS

Parents are often frustrated that their child doesn't let them know when they need to eliminate, and this is particularly true for pooping. Helping your child understand her body's internal "poop cues" can be a challenging, lengthy process. First, your child needs to develop the ability to filter out all the other exciting things she is doing in order to sense and focus on that little feeling in her tummy that says, "It's time to go." Then she has to let you know, or get herself to the potty, solo.

Tune in to your super-parent mind-reading powers to decide when she might be about to eliminate. Most children have a time of day that they often go. Remind yourself to stay close by, keep the potty handy and her diaper or pull-up off. You might even have her sit on the throne while you read her a potty book or find something entertaining to do that will keep her there for a while. When she does pee or poop, ask her how she feels now that she's gotten all that pee or poop out. Eventually, she'll start to connect that feeling of relief with getting to the potty on time.

POTTY TRICKS

- Offer to take him to the potty during the times of day when he's most likely to pee or poop.

- Place his little potty right where he likes to hide when he goes.

- Let him see his sibling or cousin using the potty like a pro.

- Make up a funny potty song together, and sing it whenever YOU have to go. Allow your mini-me to observe you doing your business, and sing, pee, and poop together. (Don't forget to record yourselves singing the song together to use in his wedding video!)

USE YOUR WORDS: SCRIPTS FOR SUCCESS

Toddlers are pros at irritating their parents. They really can't help themselves. This is going to be particularly true during toilet-training, when the laundry situation gets out of control and you feel like you're spending hours a day sitting with a small child waiting for a poop. It's a messy, frustrating, buy-carpet-cleaner-in-bulk time of life. So yes, you are going to find yourself doing all the things you swore you'd never do—scolding, yelling, threatening, huffing, puffing, swearing under your breath, and saying things shockingly similar to what YOUR parents said to you. There you are, feeling like a powerless peon under the thumb of a short, diaper-clad dictator.

I can help. I've created a few scripts for common scenarios. When you fear you might hurl a case of baby wipes right out the window, use these scripts instead. They will give you magical powers of self-control. Tape them to the bathroom mirror.

INSTEAD OF:

"What did I just step in?! Did you wet yourself AGAIN? I'm getting sick and tired of mopping up pee!"

TRY:

(Deep breath first, neutral expression.)

"Oh, you're wet. Let's get you out of these wet clothes. Next time, sing me our potty song and we can go to the bathroom together."

INSTEAD OF:

"No, no, no! Don't poop in your diaper, let's run to the potty!"

TRY:

"I notice you're pooping in your diaper. Let me know when you're done and we'll clean you up. Then I can show you how I dump the poop in the big potty."

INSTEAD OF:

"Your bed is wet AGAIN? How many times do I have to change this bed? You are getting way too old for this!"

TRY:

"It looks like your sheets are wet. I think your body is telling us it's not quite ready to be dry when you're asleep. Let's use a pull up when you sleep, so your bed will be clean and dry when you wake up. Your body will grow into being dry at night one day soon. Let's get you out of your wet clothes and into something dry."

INSTEAD OF:

"If you can't learn to use this potty, you can't go to preschool! They won't let you in! I can't go back to work if you're not at preschool. You need to learn by September first, or we are in deep trouble!"

TRY:

"Let's keep trying to learn to use the potty like a Big Kid. One day, you'll be ready. I heard there's a preschool in town that knows how to help children who are learning to use the potty. Let's go visit that school and check it out."

(And then, go and find a preschool that better understands the developmental needs of young children, which includes supporting their potty-training process.)

YOU GOT THE WIPE STUFF, BABY!

Once your child is oh, pardon the pun, a "whiz" at using the potty, it's time to start to show her how to wipe herself. Definitely take the time to work on this with her, even if it seems she's "sort of" got it. Girls have an increased risk of urinary tract infections (UTIs) at this age because of their less-than-perfect wiping techniques. In fact, instead of wiping, I recommend you teach her to "blot" after she pees. Lightly blotting herself after peeing prevents her from accidentally pulling bacteria from her bum up into her tender lady parts. Boys don't need to wipe after they pee, but should be taught to tap their penis before climbing off the potty. Remember that rap song? "Tap Your Penis"? No?

To prevent a giant pile of toilet paper on the floor every time your toddler tries to pull some off the roll, try this: squeeze your Charmin. No really, squeeze the roll so that it folds the whole thing enough that the paper can't easily cascade off. Instead, the roll will "thunk, thunk, thunk" down just a couple of squares at a time.

Wiping or tapping after a pee is one thing. But post-poop purification is a whole different situation. Post-poop wiping is a complex process that requires a lot of motor skill and coordination; so don't be surprised at how long it can take to master. For a few days (or weeks), show your child how to pull the right amount of toilet paper off the roll and get it ready for wiping. (And for you toilet-paper-folders out there, get over it. Your toddler won't be able to master that bathroom origami for quite a while.) Next, show her how to reach behind herself and wipe up toward her back. She will be tempted to wipe downward, since it's easier, so tell her in advance how you want her to wipe, and guide her hand the first several times until she gets the hang of the movement. Do explain to her why you want her to wipe this way: "If you wipe doo-doo toward your sparkly bits, you can get sick and hurt down there. You need to keep that area clean from any poo."

Post-poop wiping is a complex process that requires a lot of motor skills and coordination; so don't be surprised at how long it can take to master.

Boys also need to wipe upwards so they can make sure all the poop is cleaned off their tushies. Those flushable wet wipes are indispensible for both boys and girls—be sure to get the flushable kind. If you use regular baby wipes, you'll clog the pipes.

Teach your child to keep wiping until the TP is left clean, using a fresh wad of paper each pass until it's spotless. If there's poop on the toilet paper, great, show them that means they're doing a good job—and that it also means they need to keep wiping! This repetitive process can be frustrating for a small child (which can lead to many a skid-mark in the undies). So until your little wiper becomes an expert, be ready to help with wiping for as long as it takes. No scolding, no eye rolling—just be there as a spotter to regularly check on technique and results. Don't be surprised if this skill is developed agonizingly slowly. Many kindergarteners and first graders still need regular monitoring with wiping. As your child gets older and dexterity improves, he will be able to handle this task himself.

SOAP STARS

After the all-important flush, it's time for hand washing. Talk to your child about germs, so she understands why we scrub our hands and how we need to do it every time we use the potty. Assist with hand washing until you're sure she's gotten the hang of it. A step stool for reaching the sink helps make this process easier (and more fun). Little kids love the foamy soap dispensers and trying new scents and colors of soap at this stage.

Since potty training is such a messy business, you might want to wash toddler clothes in the extra-hot cycle of your laundry machine, and consider adding bleach. This is especially important when Junior has a case of the runs. I always keep a canister of industrial-strength surface disinfecting wipes handy in the bathroom, so I can do an extra once-over to clean up after all the lovely surprises left behind by a potty-training toddler. (Stash them up high so the kiddos can't get their hands on them, as these disinfectant-soaked wipes have strong chemicals and aren't meant for little ones to use.)

TAKING THE SHOW ON THE ROAD: TRAVEL WHILE TRAINING

Remember that your toddler's mind doesn't work like yours does. He may not even realize that potties exist in places outside your home. I still remember my daughter's amazement when she discovered that locations like the grocery store or Grandma's house also have toilets. She thought that the potties in our house were the only ones in the whole world! We take those facts for granted, but your toddler is still discovering them. So when you go out, make sure to go on a "potty seek and find" mission as soon as you get to your destination. Not only will you both learn where the bathroom is, you'll also take care of any immediate potty needs before you start your shopping, errands, or visiting.

Your little one might also be terrified of those ridiculously loud, annoyingly unpredictable automatic flushers in public bathrooms. Some experts recommend you cover the sensor with a sticky note to prevent surprise flushing. This sometimes works, but if it doesn't (like when the sticky won't stick because it has too much Cheerio dust on it from the remnants in your purse, or when the toilet flushes randomly anyway), your toddler will jump out of his skin.

If we're in a public bathroom, we make a game out of prediciting when the next toilet will flush.

Here's what we do in our family: If we're in a public bathroom, we make a game out of predicting when the next toilet will flush. I look around suspiciously and ask my toddler, "Do you hear any potties flushing? I think it's going to happen...now!" When it doesn't happen, I say, "Oh! I was wrong! Maybe you can guess! When do you think the next potty is going to flush? Now? In two seconds? In five seconds?" She makes her guess, and then we start counting. When we hear the next flush, we both say—loudly—"Loud! I hear a loud potty flushing! It's really loud!" The game combines anticipation and excitement, counting and being loud together as fun distractions from what would otherwise be a potentially unsettling situation. Don't be afraid of the reactions of others in the bathroom overhearing your loud game. Their ears are still ringing from the deafening noise of their own toilets flushing.

Consider, also, that toddlers crave familiarity. Their bodies and minds are changing every day, so any semblance of order is appreciated. Learning to do their bidness in a potty at all is still a novelty, and their own potty feels most comfortable. Asking them to use a different toilet, in a more unfamiliar setting, is a whole new level of potty training -- so don't expect it immediately.

Now if your child willingly uses the potty at preschool or day care, but refuses to do so at home, she may have gotten into a power struggle with you. It could also be caused by a disruption in the home -- if there's a new sibling, for example -- or another type of stressful change.

Another reason your child might be using the potty at day care or preschool, but not at home, is this common scenario: Perhaps your child's teacher is pressuring him to use the potty, but he's not really comfortable with it yet. So while he feels forced to use it at school, he knows he's able to make his own choices at home. Feeling more comfortable at home, your child is telling you that he's just not ready yet. Or perhaps your child's teacher has some great potty ideas that work well with your child.

Sit down for an adults-only meeting with your child's teacher and find out how the bathroom situation is handled in class, and in particular, with your child. Tell the teacher your observations and any concerns, and ask her advice. Good preschool teachers understand that children vary tremendously in their potty-learning readiness, and will happily discuss the situation with you.

TRAINING MULTIPLES:

Twins, triplets, and more—if you're raising multiples, you already know that every child will develop at his or her own pace. Potty training is no different. So while it might be a fun fantasy that your septuplets will be done with diapers simultaneously, it simply isn't likely.

Parents of multiples say that it's actually easier to train one child at a time. But if it turns out the children are all showing signs of readiness, have a little potty available for each of them to eliminate potty competition. Observe and follow each child's unique signals of readiness, and don't despair if someone is a late learner. Sometimes, the children who try to learn first actually take longer to train. The ones who start the process later might learn from watching the crowd in the bathroom and master their skills faster!

Avoid using rewards for multiples. Toddlers aren't emotionally developed enough to handle being passed over for a sticker or a piece of candy. Your child's success—and your low-key, specific praise—is enough. And of course, resist comparing your toddlers. Just as in all aspects of development, each child has different strengths and areas of challenge.

CHAPTER 4

COMPLICATIONS

"Trust yourself. You know more than you think you do."

—BENJAMIN SPOCK, M.D.

WHEN TO HOLD OFF ON POTTY TRAINING

D on't try to potty train when your child is already dealing with a lot of change. The birth of a new sibling, for example, or a move to a new home, will make potty training more stressful and difficult. I also don't recommend potty training your child when you're making a lot of other "Big Kid" transitions. I've seen families who move their child out of the crib, take away their child's bottle (or pacifier), start day care, and begin potty training—all at the same time. It just isn't a good idea and it's very likely to backfire. It's better to wait and focus on one thing at a time, like a new big kid bed, or stabilizing the family ship after a big move, before tossing a new skill in there for your kid to master. And besides, YOU don't need the extra burden of potty training when things are stressful, either. Diapers or pull-ups are much easier to use than trying to catch a resistant toddler in the act, while simultaneously nursing a newborn and making dinner. And whatever decreases your stress is good for the whole family.

IF THINGS BACK UP: CONSTIPATION

There's no standard number of times your child should poop each day or each week—it varies from child to child and sometimes from day to day. But you'll want to have a sense of his pattern, so that you can spot a problem if one arises.

Constipation usually means your child begins to poop less often, and stools become hard, "pebbly," and difficult to push out.

In more severe cases, toddlers actually have very loose, watery poop smears in their underwear or diapers; that's evidence of impacted poop, which is causing a plug in the bowel. The liquid poop oozes out around it and causes the skid marks. This is a sign of a medically serious constipation and should be treated immediately by a pediatric physician who specializes in both the medical and behavioral aspects of this problem. (I'll address chronic, severe constipation and the difficulties that can arise with it in more detail in my next book, so stay tuned!)

But even "regular" constipation is an often unrecognized and powerful enemy of potty training. When poop is trapped in the colon, it blocks the nerve signals between the abdomen and the brain, making it difficult for your child to feel whether she has to go. Surprisingly, it makes it harder for her to feel when she has to pee, too! Children can even become constipated if they poop every day, simply by not letting it all come out each time. So it's important to solve a constipation problem quickly.

Talk to your child's doctor about what is recommended, and take a good look at your family's diet, too. Loading up on the fruits and veggies and whatever other healthy foods make her go will be an important part of the solution. You can also ask the doctor if it's OK to use a little petroleum jelly around sore, reddened bum skin, and ask your doctor for directions on how to apply it. Petroleum jelly can help heal irritated skin and make pooping less painful. Painful poops can take a long time for toddlers to forget, and may result in poop-withholding, which can be really tricky to resolve.

PRESCHOOL PRESSURE: DON'T GIVE IN!

So often, I hear from parents who are stressed because their child is supposed to start preschool, and potty training is a requirement. But their kiddo is nowhere near the "complete toilet independence" that many preschools require.

Painful poops can take a long time for toddlers to forget, and may result in poop-withholding, which can be really tricky to resolve.

You might as well ask the child to drive himself to preschool. Potty training is a skill that requires developmental readiness, plus a lot of practice. These cannot be manufactured to meet an arbitrary preschool entry deadline.

Keep in mind that a good preschool makes it its business to understand the development of the children it serves—and that preschools grounded in a solid understanding of child development will have support, suggestions, and options for the three-year-old who is still learning about the potty. Also, know that many preschools have a firm "potty trained" rule on paper (based on local laws and regulations), but individual teachers may be more than willing to work with children needing support in the learning process. So quietly ask around to get "the real poop" on how potty learning is handled in the classroom.

A school's actual definition of "potty trained" can also vary quite a lot. Do they mean 100-percent, reliably, independently, no-adult-helper-required, day and night, for poop and for pee? Or does it mean "kinda-sorta" trained, will poop at home before (or after) school, but still needs a pull-up just to be on the safe side? Or, "Ninety percent potty trained, but once in a while has an oopsie?" The working definition a preschool uses may make all the difference in your decision on whether to send your child there.

DRY BY DAY, SOAKED AT NIGHT

I also get lots of questions from frustrated parents who wonder: How is it that, by day, my child is 100-percent toilet trained; yet by night, she soaks the sheets? You have to rethink this "problem," because it's simply the reality of your child's anatomical development. The potty training nerve pathways between the bladder and the brain have only recently started to develop in your child, but must grow to be strong enough that your child will be awakened from deep sleep by the urge to pee. Not only that, she must become alert enough, and motivated enough—no small feats in the middle of the night—to haul herself out of a nice, cozy bed. Then she has to either get herself into the bathroom, or holler for you to come and help her. And it's kind of dark and scary in the hallway, even with the night-light!

Many parent of bed-wetters are surprised that no amount of fluid restriction before bed seems to matter–a ton of tee-tee is still being produced at night.

On top of that, her body may not yet have developed the nighttime slowdown in urine production that eventually develops anywhere from ages two to seven. That's why many parents of bed-wetters are surprised that no amount of fluid restriction before bed seems to matter—a ton of tee-tee is still being produced at night.

There's another factor working against you: Many young children, especially ones who are very active during the daytime, sleep so deeply at night that they're difficult (or impossible) to awaken. Even if Mom or Dad is standing over them, telling them it's time to try the potty, that kid will just not wake up. So there's no way that an underdeveloped, tiny signal in the body is strong enough to rouse them. That's why day training and night training are two completely different animals. Because we're simply awaiting your child's physical development, there's no trick to speed up nighttime training, so I hope you can give your child (and yourself) a break on this one. It also may help you to know that up to 20 percent of kindergarteners still wet so frequently at night that they require a pull-up. The percentage slowly but steadily decreases each year in school, but a surprising number of children still need to wear a nighttime pull-up even into their first- and second-grade years.

It also may help you to know that up to 20 percent of kindergarteners still wet so frequently at night that they require a pull-up.

Bed-wetting is also linked to a genetic component, so if there's a parent, aunt or uncle who was a chronic bed-wetter into their school years, your child is more likely to be one, too.

But if your child was dry at night for a period of time and then regressed, that's a different story. This can be caused by medical conditions, such as a urinary tract infection, or by stress. Get to the root of the problem by discussing it with your child's doctor, and reassure your child that things will get back on track soon. Don't punish, threaten, or tease. In most cases, solving the cause of the regression will solve the bed-wetting.

How will you know when your child is ready to try ditching the diapers at night? He might be ready when he starts to wake up dry from his naps, or you might notice he isn't as wet as he used to be in the morning. Then, you can talk about his growing body to see if he's interested in sleeping without the diaper. This is a good time during potty training to start limiting fluids in the evening. You can also see if taking your child to the bathroom before YOU go to bed, at, say, 10:00 or 11:00 p.m., will help him stay dry until morning. But don't waste any effort trying before you've seen the signs of nighttime readiness, because you'll just be wasting your own precious sleep time.

Bottom line: Instead of seeing nighttime wetting as a huge problem, just relax, invest in some waterproof mattress pads and keep buying those nighttime pull-ups or diapers. By the way, I like the half-sized mattress pads that sit on top of your child's bottom sheets—this makes it easy to strip off the piddle pad, and you don't have to change the whole bed. Buy them in twos so you have a dry one on hand. The time will come when your child won't need them, I promise, and you can move on to other exciting chapters of family life. In my next book, I'll discuss some of the even more challenging potty-training issues, and I'll discuss nighttime wetness alarms and other options for night training.

BOOT CAMP: DROP AND GIVE ME A BM!

Parents often ask me about books and DVDs that promise to potty train a child in a weekend or during a "potty-training boot camp." Do these programs actually work? Not often. The few who do well over the long term with this approach tend to be "easy" personalities. This is another time it will serve you well to understand your child's temperament. Other good candidates for a "potty-training boot camp" are Accountant types, those who hate the feeling of wet or dirty diapers, and toddlers who respond well to changes.

There are many versions of this approach, but they have several things in common. First, you'll need to plan ahead and set aside all other activities in order to get the potty training done. Second, you'll be giving lots of fluids to Junior and letting him run around without pants, which will not only increase his chances of using the potty, but allow him a sneak-peek of fraternity life. Lastly, once Junior uses the potty, you'll be bestowing lots of rewards, praise, and celebration for success.

The problem is, many kids will flunk out of a potty boot camp. The approach assumes that potty training is a simple process of learning what to do with your pee and your poop. And that once your toddler learns the new routine—ta-da!—he will follow it willingly. But guess what? Most kids aren't

Accountant or "easy" types, or they don't seem to care if they're sitting tall on a steaming load, or they don't respond well to life changes. Most toddlers are fiercely addicted to their habits and routines. So potty-training boot camp is too simplistic for most children.

The other problem with this approach is that it assumes that potty training is a one-time event. The reality is this: Many toddlers can use the potty—but won't—for complicated, wacky toddler reasons that only make sense to your child. That's why potty training often takes weeks, months, or years. It's not a simple process of learning a new skill; it's about feeling in charge and in control. And usually, toddlers feel more in charge when they do things their way.

> **It's not a simple process of learning a new skill; it's about feeling in charge and in control.**

If you think your kiddo is a good candidate to try a potty-training boot camp, give it a whirl. But if you see signs of resistance and regression, that's your sign to hang up your hat, Sarge.

Now you have the straight poop on potty training. I've taken you through the basics, with lots of tricks to try. You have words to use when you get frustrated. You know about the speed bumps and potholes you might encounter along the way.

With this road map in mind, get ready: not to race, but to pace yourself, and to enjoy the magical unfolding of your child's growth and readiness that makes this momentous developmental milestone possible. When it's accomplished, your child should be proud of himself--and you should be proud of yourself, too.

Come on--let's get this potty started!

"Parenting will eventually produce bizarre behavior, and I'm not talking about the kids. Their behavior is always normal."

—BILL COSBY

WHAT IF NONE OF THIS WORKS?

I f your patience and encouragement still aren't enough, or if you hear little alarm bells going off in your mind that something is just not right, it's time to call in the pros. Don't be afraid of asking for help—your doctor, nurse, or child development specialist can really help. And don't wait, because the more complicated the potty problems get, the harder it is to make progress. Here are the signs that you need to bring your little one to the pediatrician:

- Painful poops have made him resist having a BM for more than a couple of days.

- She's turned four and you're not making progress.

- He was completely trained, and has now regressed (more than just an occasional accident).

- Long-term constipation doesn't improve with a better diet.

- There's suddenly a much more frequent need to pee.

- There's pain when peeing, or blood in the urine.

- Frequent "poop smearing" starts to happen. Your child is only pooping a small amount, with frequent "skid marks" showing up in his underwear.

Most toddlers do just great with the potty training methods I've described in this book. But if you need more tips and ideas, you're not alone. My next book, *Potty Rescue! The BabyShrink Tackles All Your Trickiest, Ickiest Potty-Training Problems*, will focus on common potty problems, including poop-withholding, chronic constipation, fears of the potty, chronic bed-wetting, and ickiest of all: poop-smearing. Also please visit my Potty Page on BabyShrink.com for more information, and don't forget to sign up for my Shrinky Thinks newsletter! You'll receive even more parenting tips and tricks, plus I'll let you know when my next book is released.

COMMONSENSE DISCLAIMER

I 'm a doctor, but not a medical doctor. I'm a doctor of psychology and a licensed psychologist, which means I'm trained and experienced in working with behavior and psychological development. Potty training is an area that encompasses parenting and psychological factors. However, medical factors can also have a major impact on your child's potty training experience and outcome, so I strongly urge you to create your potty training plan with the oversight of your child's health care provider. I'm a big believer in collaborative care, which means pediatricians, psychologists, teachers, and parents should all team up together in the best interests of your child's growth and development.

No one can replace your family's clinical health-care provider. I offer information and education about child development and general parenting issues, but can't comment on your specific family and child. I hope the insights I provide in this book, and on my website, BabyShrink.com, are helpful, but they are only for informational purposes. For specific questions pertaining to your child's health, it goes without saying: consult your pediatrician.

ACKNOWLEDGEMENTS

Because I don't want my kids to hate me for embarrassing them, I won't be thanking them in a book about potty training. No siree. Right, kids? Even if you taught me everything I know about potty training, from the trenches? Even if I love being your mom every single day?

But I will thank the love of my life, the father of my children, and my business partner, Dr. David Wittenberg, for supporting me in every one of my pursuits since the day we met more than twenty years ago. I also want to thank our parents, Peggy and Hans Krock, Joyce and Richard Wittenberg, and the late Milton Yolles, M.D.—my Dad—for their constant support and encouragement. My sister, Nora Yolles-Young, has helped me refine the BabyShrink mission and message from the beginning.

I also want to thank you, my readers and clients. You've welcomed me into your homes and lives, and I'm humbled and honored to be able to help. In turn, you've taught me innumerable lessons I'm able to share with others. YOU are the reason my first book is a potty training book. You asked for it!

And I want to thank the people who have guided and supported me professionally through the development of BabyShrink. com since 2008: Guy Kawasaki, Glenn Sakamoto, Lisa Ocasio at Learning Care Group, Adam Wilson and Meghan Hyland at Team Detroit, the whole gang at Edelman, The Parents. com team, Jill Kuramoto at KITV4, Eileen Kennedy-Moore, Ph.D., Keely Kolmes, Psy.D., Anthony DeBenedet, M.D., Cheryl Albright, Ph.D., Joseph Campos, Ph.D., Beth I. Kalish, Ph.D., Michele Borba, Ed.D., Stefanie Wilder-Taylor, Jen Singer, Shawn Burns, Danny Evans, Manoush Zomorodi, Barb Drozdowich, and my fabulous and inspirational writers group of Toby Neal, Ilima Loomis, and Linda Nagata.

And to my publishing team; Kathryn Drury Wagner, Jen Tadaki Catanzariti, Lavonne Leong, and Jing Jing Tsong: You came along at exactly the right moment to turn this book into a reality. Mahalo nui loa!

Made in the USA
Columbia, SC
10 April 2019